TABLE OF CONTENT

Contents

Introduction	5
Understanding Your Financial Landscape	8
Identifying Your Financial Goals	8
Understanding Key Financial Factors	9
Budgeting Basics: Managing Your Income and Expenses	12
Debt Management and Elimination Techniques	20
Introduction	25
Why Multiple Streams of Income?	25
Types of Income Streams	25
Building Multiple Income Streams	25
Strategies for Success	26
Overcoming Challenges	26
Maximizing Your Income Potential	27
Achieving Financial Freedom	27
Conclusion	27
Introduction	28
Understanding the Value of Money	28
Strategies for Smart Spending	28
Maximizing Value	29
Minimizing Waste	29
Cultivating Smart Spending Habits	29
Conclusion	30
Introduction	31
Understanding Insurance	31

- Estate Planning Essentials 31
- Conclusion 32
- Introduction 33
- Understanding Financial Mindset 33
- Cultivating a Wealth-Building Mentality 33
- Overcoming Limiting Beliefs and Mindset Blocks 34
- Applying Wealth-Building Principles 34
- Embracing a Wealth-Building Lifestyle 34
- Conclusion: Empowering Your Financial Future 35
- Introduction 36
- Understanding Financial Obstacles 36
- Building Financial Resilience 37
- Strategies for Long-Term Financial Success 37
- Overcoming Psychological Barriers 37
- Conclusion 37
- Introduction 38
- Understanding Retirement Planning 38
- Creating a Retirement Plan 38
- Generating Retirement Income 38
- Wealth Preservation Strategies 39
- Estate Planning Considerations 39
- Conclusion: 39
- Building a Legacy: Charitable Giving and Philanthropy 40
- Introduction 40
- Understanding Philanthropy 40
- Strategies for Effective Giving 40
- Legacy Planning through Philanthropy 41

Engaging Family and Community 41

Conclusion 41

Money and Relationships: Navigating Financial Conversations with Loved Ones 42

Introduction 42

Understanding the Impact of Money on Relationships 42

Building Financial Intimacy 42

Addressing Money Conflicts 42

Money and Relationship Milestones 43

Supporting Each Other Financially 43

Balancing Independence and Interdependence 43

Planning for the Future 43

Navigating Financial Challenges Together 43

Celebrating Financial Milestones 44

Conclusion 44

Money Mastery: Take Control of Your Finances and Your Future

" Empower Your Finances, Shape Your Destiny: Master Money, Secure Your Future"

Author Bio:

Divya Dharshan

Introduction

Welcome to "Money Mastery: Take Control of Your Finances and Your Future"! In this book, we embark on a journey toward financial empowerment and mastery. Money plays a crucial role in our lives, influencing our ability to achieve our goals, fulfill our dreams, and live the life we desire. Yet, many of us struggle with managing our finances effectively, feeling overwhelmed by bills, debt, and financial uncertainty.

The purpose of this book is to provide you with the knowledge, strategies, and mindset shifts necessary to take control of your financial destiny. Whether you're just starting your financial journey or seeking to improve your existing financial situation, this book is designed to equip you with the tools and insights needed to build a solid foundation for financial success.

Throughout the chapters that follow, we'll explore key principles of personal finance, including budgeting, saving, investing, debt management, passive income generation, and more. You'll learn how to set SMART financial goals, develop a personalized budget, make informed investment decisions, and protect your assets for the future.

But mastering money isn't just about crunching numbers and following financial rules. It's also about cultivating the right mindset and attitudes toward money. That's why we'll delve into the importance of financial mindset and how to overcome common psychological barriers that may be holding you back from achieving your financial goals.

Additionally, we'll address the role of money in relationships and provide guidance on navigating financial conversations with loved ones. Whether you're managing finances as a couple, teaching your children about money, or planning for retirement together, effective communication and shared financial goals are essential for success.

As we embark on this journey together, I encourage you to approach each chapter with an open mind and a willingness to take action. Remember, financial mastery is not achieved overnight—it's a continuous process of learning, adapting, and making informed decisions. By applying the principles outlined in this book and taking proactive steps toward financial empowerment, you'll be well on your way to creating a brighter financial future for yourself and your loved ones.

Now, let's begin our journey toward money mastery together.

Understanding Your Financial Landscape

Before you can embark on the journey toward financial mastery, it's essential to gain a clear understanding of your current financial landscape. This chapter will guide you through the process of assessing your financial situation, identifying your financial goals, and understanding the key factors that impact your financial health.

Assessing Your Financial Situation

The first step in mastering your money is to take stock of your current financial situation. This involves gathering information about your income, expenses, assets, and liabilities. By understanding where you stand financially, you can make informed decisions about how to move forward.

Calculate Your Net Worth: Your net worth is the difference between your assets (what you own) and your liabilities (what you owe). Calculate your net worth by listing all your assets and subtracting your liabilities. This will give you a clear picture of your overall financial position.

Track Your Income and Expenses: Keep track of your income sources and all your expenses, including fixed expenses (such as rent or mortgage payments) and variable expenses (such as groceries and entertainment). This will help you understand where your money is going each month and identify areas where you can cut back or optimize your spending.

Review Your Credit Report: Your credit report contains information about your credit history, including any outstanding debts, payment history, and credit inquiries. Reviewing your credit report regularly can help you identify any errors or discrepancies that may be affecting your credit score.

Identifying Your Financial Goals

Once you have a clear understanding of your current financial situation, the next step is to identify your financial goals. Financial goals provide a roadmap for your financial journey and serve as a benchmark for measuring your progress. When setting financial goals, it's essential to make them specific, measurable, achievable, relevant, and time-bound (SMART).

Short-Term Goals:

Short-term goals are those you aim to achieve within the next one to three years. Examples include building an emergency fund, paying off credit card debt, or saving for a vacation.

Medium-Term Goals:

Medium-term goals typically have a timeframe of three to five years and may include buying a car, saving for a down payment on a home, or funding a child's education.

Long-Term Goals:

Long-term goals are those you hope to achieve in five or more years. These may include retirement planning, saving for children's college education, or purchasing a second home.

Understanding Key Financial Factors

Finally, it's essential to understand the key factors that impact your financial health. These factors include your income, expenses, savings rate, debt-to-income ratio, credit score, and investment performance. By monitoring these factors regularly and making adjustments as needed, you can stay on track toward achieving your financial goals.

In the next chapter, we'll explore strategies for budgeting and saving, laying the foundation for a strong financial future. Remember, understanding your financial landscape is the first step toward financial mastery, so take the time to assess your situation and set clear goals for the road ahead.

Setting SMART Financial Goals

In the journey towards financial independence and security, setting clear and achievable goals is paramount. The SMART criteria — Specific, Measurable, Achievable, Relevant, and Time-bound — provide a framework for crafting goals that are not only meaningful but also actionable.

Understanding SMART Goals

Specific:

Your financial goals should be clear and well-defined. Instead of saying "I want to save money," specify how much you want to save and for what purpose.

Measurable:

You should be able to track your progress and know when you've achieved your goal. This could involve setting a target amount to save or a specific debt to pay off.

Achievable:

While it's important to dream big, your goals should also be realistic given your current financial situation. Setting unattainable goals can lead to frustration and disappointment.

Relevant:

Your financial goals should align with your values and priorities. Ask yourself why each goal is important to you and how it fits into your overall financial plan.

Time-bound:

Set deadlines for achieving your goals to create a sense of urgency and accountability. Without a timeframe, goals can easily be pushed aside and forgotten.

Identifying Your Financial Goals

Start by identifying what matters most to you financially. This could include saving for retirement, buying a home, paying off debt, or funding your children's education. Break down your goals into short-term, medium-term, and long-term objectives.

Defining SMART Goals

Once you've identified your financial goals, it's time to make them SMART:

- Specific: Clearly define what you want to achieve. For example, instead of saying "I want to save money," specify how much you want to save and what you're saving for.
- Measurable: Determine how you will track your progress. This could involve monitoring your savings account balance, tracking your debt repayment, or measuring your investment returns.
- Achievable: Ensure that your goals are within reach given your current financial resources and circumstances. If necessary, break larger goals into smaller, more manageable steps.
- Relevant: Consider how each goal aligns with your values, priorities, and long-term objectives. Focus on goals that will have the greatest impact on your financial well-being.
- Time-bound: Set deadlines for achieving each goal. This could be a specific date or time frame by which you want to accomplish your objective.

Examples of SMART Financial Goals

Here are some examples of SMART financial goals:

- Paying off $5,000 in credit card debt within 12 months.
- Saving $10,000 for a down payment on a home within 3 years.
- Increasing monthly retirement contributions by 10% within 6 months.

By following the SMART criteria, you can create financial goals that are clear, achievable, and aligned with your long-term objectives. Remember to regularly review and adjust your goals as your financial situation evolves.

Budgeting Basics: Managing Your Income and Expenses

Budgeting is a fundamental financial skill that empowers individuals to take control of their money and achieve their financial goals. By creating a budget, you can track your income, prioritize your spending, and make informed decisions about your finances. In this guide, we'll explore the basics of budgeting and provide practical tips for managing your income and expenses effectively.

Understanding the Importance of Budgeting

A budget serves as a roadmap for your financial journey, helping you allocate your resources in a way that aligns with your goals and priorities. Whether you're saving for a major purchase, paying off debt, or planning for retirement, a budget provides the framework for achieving your objectives.

Creating a Budget

Calculate Your Income:
Start by determining your total monthly income, including wages, salary, bonuses, and any other sources of income.

List Your Expenses:
Next, make a list of all your monthly expenses, including fixed expenses (e.g., rent, mortgage, utilities) and variable expenses (e.g., groceries, dining out, entertainment). Differentiate Between Needs and Wants: Differentiate between essential expenses (needs) and discretionary expenses (wants). Prioritize your needs and allocate funds accordingly.

Set Financial Goals:
Identify your short-term and long-term financial goals. These could include building an emergency fund, paying off debt, or saving for a vacation.

Allocate Funds:

Allocate a portion of your income towards each expense category based on your priorities and financial goals.

Track Your Spending:

Keep track of your expenses throughout the month to ensure that you're staying within your budget. Use apps or spreadsheets to monitor your spending and identify areas where you can cut back.

Tips for Effective Budgeting

- Be Realistic: Set realistic expectations for your budget and allow for some flexibility. It's okay to adjust your budget as needed to accommodate unexpected expenses or changes in income.

- Review Regularly: Review your budget regularly to assess your progress and make any necessary adjustments. Life circumstances and financial goals may change over time, so it's important to keep your budget up to date.

- Pay Yourself First: Prioritize saving by allocating a portion of your income towards savings and investments before paying for other expenses.

- Plan for Emergencies: Build an emergency fund to cover unexpected expenses, such as medical bills or car repairs. Aim to save enough to cover three to six months' worth of living expenses.

- Seek Professional Advice: If you're struggling to create or stick to a budget, consider seeking help from a financial advisor or counselor. They can provide personalized guidance and support to help you reach your financial goals.

This comprehensive guide provides a detailed overview of budgeting basics, including the importance of budgeting, steps for creating a budget, practical tips for effective budgeting, and strategies for achieving financial goals. It aims to empower readers with the knowledge and tools they need to take control of their finances and build a secure financial future.

Saving Strategies for Financial Security

Introduction

In today's uncertain economic climate, saving money has never been more critical. Whether you're looking to build an emergency fund, save for retirement, or achieve other financial goals, having a solid savings strategy is essential for long-term financial security. In this guide, we'll explore various saving strategies that can help you take control of your finances and build a brighter financial future.

Assessing Your Financial Situation

Before diving into saving strategies, it's essential to assess your current financial situation. Take stock of your income, expenses, debts, and assets to get a clear picture of where you stand financially. Identify your financial goals and priorities, whether it's saving for a down payment on a house, paying off debt, or building a retirement nest egg. Understanding your financial landscape is the first step toward creating an effective savings plan.

Building an Emergency Fund

One of the most critical aspects of financial security is having an emergency fund. An emergency fund acts as a financial safety net, providing you with a buffer in case of unexpected expenses or income loss. Aim to save enough to cover three to six months' worth of living expenses in your emergency fund. Start by setting small, achievable savings goals and gradually increase the amount as you're able.

Automating Your Savings

Automating your savings is a powerful way to make saving money effortless. Set up automatic transfers from your checking account to your savings account each month. You can also use apps and tools that round up your purchases to the nearest dollar and deposit the spare change into your savings account. By automating your savings, you'll be less tempted to spend the money and more likely to reach your savings goals.

Paying Yourself First

Paying yourself first means prioritizing saving money before paying your other expenses. Treat your savings like a non-negotiable expense, just like your rent or mortgage. Set aside a portion of your income for savings as soon as you get paid, before allocating money for other expenses. By making saving a priority, you'll ensure that you're consistently putting money away for your future financial goals.

Cutting Expenses and Increasing Income

To boost your savings, consider cutting expenses and increasing your income. Look for areas where you can reduce discretionary spending, such as dining out less frequently or canceling subscription services you don't use. Additionally, explore opportunities to increase your income, such as taking on a side hustle or freelance work. By reducing expenses and boosting income, you'll have more money available to put toward your savings goals.

Setting Savings Goals

Setting specific, measurable, achievable, relevant, and time-bound (SMART) goals is essential for staying on track with your savings. Break down your larger financial goals into smaller, actionable steps and set deadlines for achieving each milestone. Regularly review your progress and adjust your goals as needed. Having clear savings goals will help you stay motivated and focused on your financial objectives.

Investing for the Future

While saving money is crucial, investing can help your savings grow over time. Consider investing in a diversified portfolio of stocks, bonds, and other assets to build wealth and achieve your long-term financial goals. Start with small investments and gradually increase your contributions as your financial situation allows. Keep in mind that investing carries risks, so be sure to do your research and consult with a financial advisor if needed.

Reviewing and Adjusting Your Saving Strategies

Finally, it's essential to regularly review and adjust your saving strategies as needed. Life circumstances and financial goals can change over time, so it's essential to stay flexible and adapt your savings plan accordingly. Celebrate your successes along the way and use any setbacks as learning opportunities to refine your approach. By staying proactive and engaged with your finances, you'll be better equipped to achieve long-term financial security.

Conclusion

Saving money is a crucial step toward achieving financial security and building wealth. By following these saving strategies and staying disciplined in your approach, you can take control of your finances and create a brighter financial future for yourself and your family. Remember, it's never too late to start saving, so take action today and begin working toward your financial goals.

Investing Fundamentals: Building Wealth for the Future

Introduction

Investing is a powerful tool for building wealth and achieving financial goals. Whether you're saving for retirement, funding your children's education, or building a nest egg for the future, investing can help you grow your money over time. In this guide, we'll explore the fundamentals of investing and provide you with the knowledge and tools you need to become a successful investor.

Understanding the Basics of Investing

Before diving into the world of investing, it's essential to understand the basics. Investing involves putting money into financial assets with the expectation of generating a return on your investment. There are various types of investments, including stocks, bonds, mutual funds, exchange-traded funds (ETFs), real estate, and more. Each investment comes with its own level of risk and potential return, so it's essential to do your research and understand the characteristics of each asset class.

Setting Investment Goals

One of the first steps in investing is setting clear investment goals. Ask yourself what you're investing for and what you hope to achieve with your investments. Are you saving for retirement, planning to buy a home, or looking to build wealth over the long term? By defining your investment goals, you can tailor your investment strategy to meet your specific needs and objectives.

Assessing Your Risk Tolerance

Understanding your risk tolerance is another crucial aspect of investing. Risk tolerance refers to your willingness and ability to endure fluctuations in the value of your investments. Generally, investments with higher potential returns also come with higher levels of risk. Assess your risk tolerance based on factors such as your investment timeframe, financial goals, and comfort level with volatility. A conservative investor may prefer lower-risk investments like bonds, while a more aggressive investor may be comfortable with higher-risk, higher-reward options like stocks.

Diversification: Spreading Your Risk

Diversification is a key principle of investing that involves spreading your investment across different asset classes, industries, and geographic regions. By diversifying your portfolio, you can reduce the impact of any single investment's performance on your overall portfolio. Diversification helps mitigate risk and can enhance returns over the long term. Consider building a diversified portfolio that includes a mix of stocks, bonds, real estate, and other asset classes to achieve optimal risk-adjusted returns.

Asset Allocation: Finding the Right Mix

Asset allocation refers to how you distribute your investment portfolio among different asset classes. Your asset allocation should align with your investment goals, risk tolerance, and investment timeframe. A well-balanced asset allocation can help you achieve a desirable level of return while minimizing risk. Consider factors such as your age, financial goals, and risk tolerance when determining the optimal asset allocation for your portfolio.

Investing Strategies and Approaches

There are various investment strategies and approaches you can use to build wealth over time. Some investors prefer a passive approach, such as investing in index funds or ETFs that track broad market indices. Others may prefer an active approach, where they actively buy and sell individual stocks or bonds in an attempt to outperform the market. Whichever approach you choose, be sure to do your research and stick to a disciplined investment strategy that aligns with your goals and risk tolerance.

Monitoring and Rebalancing Your Portfolio

Once you've built your investment portfolio, it's essential to monitor its performance regularly and make adjustments as needed. Review your portfolio periodically to ensure it remains aligned with your investment goals and risk tolerance. Rebalance your portfolio as necessary to maintain your desired asset allocation and risk level. Regular monitoring and rebalancing can help you stay on track toward achieving your long-term financial goals.

Investing for the Long Term

Investing is a long-term endeavor, and success often requires patience, discipline, and a long-term perspective. Avoid trying to time the market or chasing short-term gains, as this can lead to costly mistakes. Instead, focus on building a well-diversified portfolio tailored to your investment goals and risk tolerance. Stay disciplined in your approach, and remember that investing is a marathon, not a sprint.

Conclusion

Investing is an essential tool for building wealth and achieving financial goals over the long term. By understanding the fundamentals of investing, setting clear investment goals, and following a disciplined investment strategy, you can increase your chances of success as an investor. Remember to diversify your portfolio, monitor your investments regularly, and stay focused on the long term. With patience, discipline, and a solid investment plan, you can build wealth for the future and achieve financial security for yourself and your family.

Debt Management and Elimination Techniques

Introduction

Debt can be a significant source of stress and financial burden for many individuals and families. Whether it's credit card debt, student loans, or mortgages, carrying debt can hinder your ability to achieve financial goals and lead to long-term financial instability. In this guide, we'll explore various debt management and elimination techniques to help you take control of your finances and work towards a debt-free future.

Understanding Your Debt

The first step in effective debt management is understanding your current debt situation. Take inventory of all your debts, including the type of debt, outstanding balances, interest rates, and minimum monthly payments. Creating a detailed list of your debts will give you a clear picture of your financial obligations and help you develop a strategy for paying them off.

Prioritizing Your Debts

Once you've identified all your debts, it's essential to prioritize them based on factors such as interest rates, loan terms, and outstanding balances. High-interest debt, such as credit card debt, should typically be prioritized over lower-interest debt like student loans or mortgages. By focusing on paying off high-interest debt first, you can save money on interest payments and accelerate your journey towards debt freedom.

Creating a Budget

A budget is a powerful tool for managing your finances and paying off debt. Start by tracking your income and expenses to understand where your money is going each month. Identify areas where you can cut back on discretionary spending and allocate more money towards debt repayment. By creating a realistic budget and sticking to it, you can free up more money to put towards paying off your debts.

Snowball vs. Avalanche Method

Two popular debt repayment strategies are the snowball method and the avalanche method. With the snowball method, you focus on paying off your smallest debts first while making minimum payments on larger debts. Once the smallest debt is paid off, you roll the money you were paying towards that debt into paying off the next smallest debt, and so on. This method can provide a psychological boost by seeing quick wins early in the process.

On the other hand, the avalanche method involves prioritizing debts based on interest rates, starting with the debt with the highest interest rate. You focus on paying off high-interest debt first while making minimum payments on lower-interest debt. While the avalanche method may save you more money on interest payments in the long run, it can take longer to see progress compared to the snowball method.

Debt Consolidation

Debt consolidation involves combining multiple debts into a single loan with a lower interest rate, typically through a personal loan or balance transfer credit card. Consolidating your debts can simplify your finances and potentially save you money on interest payments. However, it's essential to carefully consider the terms and fees associated with any debt consolidation option and ensure that it aligns with your financial goals.

Negotiating with Creditors

If you're struggling to keep up with your debt payments, don't hesitate to reach out to your creditors to discuss your situation. Many creditors are willing to work with borrowers to establish more manageable repayment plans or negotiate lower interest rates. Be proactive in communicating with your creditors and exploring options for debt relief.

Seeking Professional Help

If you're overwhelmed by debt and struggling to make progress on your own, it may be beneficial to seek professional help from a credit counselor or debt relief agency. These professionals can provide personalized advice and guidance tailored to your unique financial situation. They can help you develop a debt repayment plan, negotiate with creditors on your behalf, and explore options for debt relief, such as debt settlement or bankruptcy.

Staying Committed to Your Plan

Finally, staying committed to your debt repayment plan is essential for achieving long-term success. It's normal to encounter setbacks and challenges along the way, but don't get discouraged. Stay focused on your goals, celebrate your progress, and keep moving forward one step at a time. With determination, discipline, and a solid debt management strategy, you can take control of your finances and work towards a debt-free future.

Conclusion

Debt management and elimination require careful planning, discipline, and commitment. By understanding your debt, creating a budget, prioritizing your debts, and exploring debt repayment strategies like the snowball method or avalanche method, you can take significant steps towards financial freedom. Don't hesitate to seek professional help if you're struggling to manage your debt on your own. With perseverance and determination, you can overcome debt and build a brighter financial future for yourself and your family.

Mastering the Art of Passive Income

Introduction

Passive income is a powerful wealth-building tool that allows you to generate money with minimal ongoing effort or maintenance. Unlike active income, which requires your direct involvement in exchange for payment, passive income streams continue to generate revenue even when you're not actively working. In this guide, we'll explore various strategies for mastering the art of passive income and building a more secure financial future.

Understanding Passive Income

Passive income is income that you earn without actively working for it on a regular basis. It's money generated from assets you own or investments you've made that require minimal effort to maintain. Common sources of passive income include rental properties, dividend-paying stocks, interest from savings accounts or bonds, royalties from intellectual property, and income from online businesses or affiliate marketing. Passive income streams can provide financial security, flexibility, and freedom by diversifying your sources of income and reducing reliance on active employment.

Building Passive Income Streams

There are many different ways to generate passive income, and the key is to find the strategies that align with your skills, interests, and financial goals. Real estate investing is one popular option for building passive income through rental properties or real estate investment trusts (REITs). Dividend investing involves purchasing stocks of companies that pay regular dividends to shareholders. Peer-to-peer lending platforms allow you to earn interest by lending money to individuals or businesses. Creating digital products, such as ebooks, online courses, or software, can generate passive income through sales or licensing agreements. Affiliate marketing involves promoting other people's products or services and earning a commission for each sale or lead generated.

Evaluating Passive Income Opportunities

When considering different passive income opportunities, it's essential to conduct thorough research and due diligence to evaluate the potential risks and rewards. Consider factors such as the initial investment required, ongoing maintenance or management responsibilities, expected returns, and scalability. Look for opportunities that offer a balance of passive income potential and alignment with your long-term financial goals. Diversifying your passive income streams across multiple sources can help spread risk and increase overall stability.

Overcoming Common Challenges

While passive income can offer significant benefits, it's not without its challenges. Building passive income streams often requires patience, persistence, and a willingness to learn from failures or setbacks. It's essential to have realistic expectations and understand that building passive income takes time and effort upfront. Be prepared to invest in yourself through education, training, or mentorship to develop the skills and knowledge needed to succeed. Stay disciplined and focused on your goals, and don't be afraid to adapt your strategy as needed based on changing market conditions or personal circumstances.

Maximizing Passive Income Potential

Once you've established passive income streams, focus on maximizing their potential by optimizing your assets and investments. Continuously monitor and evaluate your passive income sources to identify opportunities for growth or improvement. Consider reinvesting profits into additional income-generating assets to accelerate your wealth-building efforts. Explore strategies for passive income automation, such as hiring property management companies or leveraging technology to streamline business operations. Stay informed about industry trends and emerging opportunities to stay ahead of the curve and capitalize on new passive income possibilities.

Conclusion

Mastering the art of passive income requires a combination of creativity, resourcefulness, and strategic planning. By diversifying your income streams, evaluating opportunities, overcoming challenges, and maximizing your passive income potential, you can build a more secure financial future and achieve greater financial freedom. Remember that passive income is not a get-rich-quick scheme but rather a long-term wealth-building strategy that requires patience, persistence, and dedication. With the right mindset and approach, you can unlock the power of passive income and create the lifestyle you desire.

Creating Multiple Streams of Income

Introduction

In today's rapidly changing economy, creating multiple streams of income has become essential for financial security and flexibility. This guide will explore the concept of multiple streams of income, why they are important, and strategies for building diverse income streams to achieve your financial goals.

Why Multiple Streams of Income?

Relying solely on a single source of income, such as a job or traditional business, can leave you vulnerable to financial instability. Multiple streams of income provide a safety net, spreading risk and ensuring that you have alternative sources of revenue in case one stream dries up. Additionally, having multiple income streams can increase your earning potential and help you achieve financial freedom by diversifying your sources of revenue.

Types of Income Streams

There are various types of income streams you can create, including:

- Active Income: Income earned through active work, such as a salary from a job or income from a freelance business.
- Passive Income: Income generated with minimal ongoing effort, such as rental income, dividends from stocks, or royalties from intellectual property.
- Portfolio Income: Income generated from investments, such as interest from savings accounts, capital gains from selling stocks, or dividends from mutual funds.
- Residual Income: Income earned repeatedly from a single effort, such as affiliate marketing commissions or royalties from book sales.

Building Multiple Income Streams

1. Diversify Your Skills and Talents

Identify your skills, talents, and interests, and explore ways to monetize them. Consider freelancing, consulting, teaching, or providing services in areas where you excel.

2: Invest in Income-Generating Assets

Invest in assets that generate passive income, such as rental properties, dividend-paying stocks, peer-to-peer lending platforms, or digital products.

3: Start a Side Business

Launch a side business based on your passions or hobbies. Explore opportunities in e-commerce, dropshipping, affiliate marketing, or creating and selling handmade products.

Strategies for Success

4: Leverage the Power of the Internet

Harness the internet to reach a global audience and expand your income-generating opportunities. Explore online marketplaces, affiliate programs, and digital platforms to monetize your skills and expertise.

5: Create Multiple Income Streams within Each Category

Diversify within each category of income to spread risk and maximize your earning potential. For example, if you're investing in real estate, consider owning properties in different locations or investing in different types of properties, such as residential, commercial, or vacation rentals.

6: Focus on Scalability and Passive Income

Prioritize income streams that offer scalability and the potential for passive income. Look for opportunities to automate or outsource repetitive tasks to free up your time and focus on expanding your income streams.

Overcoming Challenges

Building multiple streams of income requires dedication, resilience, and a willingness to take risks. Be prepared to face challenges such as time constraints, financial limitations, and uncertainty. Stay focused on your goals, adapt to changing circumstances, and continuously seek opportunities for growth and improvement.

Maximizing Your Income Potential

7: Monitor and Evaluate Your Income Streams Regularly

Keep track of your income streams and analyze their performance regularly. Identify areas for improvement, capitalize on successful strategies, and pivot when necessary to optimize your earning potential.

8: Reinvest Profits for Growth

Reinvest a portion of your earnings into expanding your income-generating activities. Consider reinvesting profits into new ventures, acquiring additional assets, or scaling up existing businesses to accelerate your wealth-building efforts.

Achieving Financial Freedom

9: Set Clear Financial Goals

Define your financial goals and develop a plan to achieve them. Set specific, measurable, achievable, relevant, and time-bound (SMART) goals to guide your efforts and track your progress over time.

10: Build Resilience and Adaptability

Cultivate resilience and adaptability to navigate challenges and setbacks along the way. Stay flexible and open-minded, embrace change, and be willing to pivot your strategies as needed to stay on course toward financial freedom.

Conclusion

Creating multiple streams of income is a powerful strategy for achieving financial security, flexibility, and freedom. By diversifying your sources of revenue, leveraging your skills and talents, and embracing new opportunities, you can build a more stable and prosperous financial future. Remember that success takes time, effort, and persistence, but with determination and perseverance, you can unlock the potential of multiple income streams and create the lifestyle you desire.

Smart Spending: Maximizing Value and Minimizing Waste

Introduction

Smart spending is the art of making informed financial decisions that maximize value and minimize waste. In today's consumer-driven society, it's easy to fall into the trap of overspending on unnecessary items or impulse purchases. This guide will explore the principles of smart spending, strategies for making wise purchasing decisions, and tips for optimizing your budget to achieve your financial goals.

Understanding the Value of Money

1. Assessing Needs vs. Wants

Distinguish between essential needs and discretionary wants to prioritize your spending effectively. Focus on fulfilling your basic needs such as food, shelter, and healthcare before indulging in non-essential purchases.

2. Evaluating Long-Term Benefits

Consider the long-term value of your purchases rather than just the immediate gratification. Invest in items or experiences that offer lasting benefits and align with your goals and priorities.

Strategies for Smart Spending

3. Setting a Budget

Establish a realistic budget based on your income, expenses, and financial goals. Allocate funds for essential expenses, savings, and discretionary spending categories, and track your spending to stay within your budgetary limits.

4. Researching Before Buying

Conduct thorough research before making major purchases to compare prices, read reviews, and identify the best deals. Take advantage of price comparison websites, consumer reviews, and product specifications to make informed decisions.

Maximizing Value

5. Seeking Discounts and Deals

Look for discounts, coupons, and promotional offers to save money on your purchases. Explore online coupon websites, sign up for retailer newsletters, and consider joining loyalty programs to access exclusive discounts and rewards.

6. Negotiating Prices

Don't be afraid to negotiate prices, especially when making large purchases or dealing with independent sellers. Politely inquire about discounts, price matching, or bundling deals to lower the cost and maximize your savings.

Minimizing Waste

7. Practicing Mindful Consumption

Avoid impulse buying and unnecessary purchases by practicing mindful consumption. Pause and reflect on whether a purchase aligns with your needs, values, and budget before making a buying decision.

8. Adopting Sustainable Habits

Reduce waste and environmental impact by choosing sustainable and eco-friendly products whenever possible. Opt for reusable items, minimize packaging waste, and support brands that prioritize ethical and sustainable practices.

Cultivating Smart Spending Habits

9. Avoiding Lifestyle Inflation

Resist the temptation to increase your spending as your income grows. Instead, focus on maintaining or improving your standard of living while saving and investing for the future.

10. Practicing Delayed Gratification

Practice delayed gratification by postponing non-essential purchases and saving up for larger goals or experiences. Delaying gratification can help you avoid impulse buying and make more intentional spending decisions.

Conclusion

Smart spending is a fundamental skill that can help you achieve financial stability, reduce stress, and build a brighter financial future. By adopting principles of mindful consumption, setting a budget, maximizing value, and minimizing waste, you can make informed financial decisions that align with your goals and values. Remember that smart spending is not about depriving yourself but rather about making choices that support your long-term financial well-being.

Protecting Your Assets: Insurance and Estate Planning

Introduction

Protecting your assets is an essential aspect of financial planning to safeguard your wealth and secure your legacy for future generations. Insurance and estate planning are two crucial components of asset protection that help mitigate risks, minimize financial losses, and ensure your assets are distributed according to your wishes. This guide explores the importance of insurance and estate planning, key strategies for asset protection, and how to safeguard your financial well-being for the long term.

Understanding Insurance

1: Types of Insurance Coverage

- Life Insurance: Provides financial protection for your loved ones in the event of your death, helping to cover expenses such as funeral costs, mortgage payments, and living expenses.
- Health Insurance: Offers coverage for medical expenses, including doctor visits, hospitalization, prescription drugs, and preventive care, helping to manage healthcare costs and protect against unexpected medical bills.
- Property and Casualty Insurance: Protects against property damage, theft, liability claims, and other risks associated with homeownership, rental properties, and personal belongings.

2: Assessing Your Insurance Needs

Evaluate your financial situation, lifestyle, and risk tolerance to determine the types and amount of insurance coverage you need. Consider factors such as your age, health, income, dependents, assets, and liabilities when selecting insurance policies to ensure adequate protection for yourself and your family.

Estate Planning Essentials

3: Importance of Estate Planning

Estate planning involves the process of creating a comprehensive plan for the management and distribution of your assets upon your death or incapacity. It allows you to specify your wishes regarding asset distribution, guardianship of minor children, healthcare decisions, and other important matters, minimizing confusion, conflicts, and legal challenges for your heirs.

4. Components of Estate Planning

- Will: A legal document that outlines how you want your assets to be distributed after your death and appoints an executor to oversee the administration of your estate.
- Trust: A fiduciary arrangement that allows a trustee to hold and manage assets on behalf of beneficiaries according to the terms specified in the trust document, providing flexibility, privacy, and control over asset distribution.
- Power of Attorney: Authorizes a designated individual (attorney-in-fact) to make financial or healthcare decisions on your behalf if you become incapacitated or unable to manage your affairs.

Conclusion

Protecting your assets through insurance and estate planning is essential for ensuring financial security, minimizing risks, and preserving your legacy for future generations. By assessing your insurance needs, selecting appropriate coverage, and creating a comprehensive estate plan, you can safeguard your assets, provide for your loved ones, and achieve peace of mind knowing your affairs are in order.

Financial Mindset: Cultivating a Wealth-Building Mentality

Introduction

Developing a financial mindset focused on wealth-building is essential for achieving long-term financial success and independence. Your mindset shapes your beliefs, attitudes, and behaviors toward money, influencing how you manage finances, make decisions, and pursue financial goals. This guide explores the concept of a wealth-building mentality, strategies for cultivating a positive financial mindset, and the transformative impact it can have on your financial well-being.

Understanding Financial Mindset

1. Defining a Wealth-Building Mentality

A wealth-building mentality involves adopting beliefs, habits, and attitudes that support financial growth, abundance, and prosperity. It encompasses traits such as optimism, perseverance, discipline, and a willingness to take calculated risks to achieve financial goals.

2. Shifting Your Money Mindset

- From Scarcity to Abundance: Replace scarcity-based thinking with abundance mindset, focusing on opportunities, possibilities, and abundance rather than limitations and scarcity.
- From Consumerism to Financial Independence: Transition from a consumer mindset centered on instant gratification and material possessions to a mindset focused on financial independence, wealth creation, and long-term prosperity.

Cultivating a Wealth-Building Mentality

3. Strategies for Developing a Positive Financial Mindset

- **Set Clear Financial Goals:** Define specific, measurable, achievable, relevant, and time-bound (SMART) financial goals to provide direction, motivation, and focus for your wealth-building efforts.
- **Practice Gratitude and Visualization:** Cultivate gratitude for what you have and visualize your financial goals as already accomplished, harnessing the power of positive thinking and visualization to manifest desired outcomes.
- **Educate Yourself:** Invest in financial education to enhance your knowledge, skills, and confidence in managing money, making informed decisions, and navigating financial markets effectively.

Overcoming Limiting Beliefs and Mindset Blocks

4. Identifying and Overcoming Financial Mindset Blocks

- **Fear of Failure:** Embrace failure as a learning opportunity and stepping stone to success, reframing setbacks as valuable lessons that propel you closer to your financial goals.
- **Scarcity Mentality:** Challenge scarcity-based beliefs and adopt an abundance mindset, recognizing and appreciating the abundance of opportunities, resources, and possibilities available to you.

Applying Wealth-Building Principles

5. Principles of Wealth Accumulation

- **Live Below Your Means:** Practice frugality, budgeting, and conscious spending to ensure that your expenses are lower than your income, allowing you to save, invest, and build wealth over time.
- **Invest Wisely:** Diversify your investment portfolio, minimize risks, and leverage compounding returns to grow your wealth steadily and sustainably.
- **Think Long-Term:** Adopt a long-term perspective on wealth accumulation, focusing on consistency, patience, and persistence in pursuing your financial goals.

Embracing a Wealth-Building Lifestyle

6. Integrating Wealth-Building Practices into Your Daily Life

- **Mindful Spending:** Make conscious choices about how you allocate your financial resources, prioritizing spending on essentials and investments that align with your values and goals.

- Continuous Learning: Commit to lifelong learning and personal development, seeking opportunities to expand your financial knowledge, skills, and mindset.

Conclusion: Empowering Your Financial Future

Cultivating a wealth-building mentality is not just about accumulating money; it's about transforming your relationship with money and empowering yourself to create the life you desire. By adopting a positive financial mindset, setting clear goals, overcoming limiting beliefs, and applying wealth-building principles in your daily life, you can take control of your financial future, build lasting wealth, and achieve financial freedom.

Overcoming Financial Obstacles and Challenges

Introduction

In the journey towards financial freedom and security, it's common to encounter various obstacles and challenges that can hinder progress and derail plans. However, with the right mindset, strategies, and resilience, it's possible to overcome these obstacles and emerge stronger and more financially empowered. This guide delves into the common financial obstacles individuals face, explores effective strategies for overcoming them, and offers insights to help you navigate challenges on your path to financial success.

Understanding Financial Obstacles

1. Identifying Common Financial Challenges

Financial obstacles can manifest in various forms, including:

- Debt Burden: Excessive debt can weigh heavily on finances, making it challenging to save, invest, and achieve financial goals.
- Insufficient Income: Low wages, unemployment, or underemployment may limit your ability to cover expenses, save, or invest for the future.

Overcoming Financial Challenges

2. Strategies for Financial Resilience

- Budgeting and Expense Management: Create a realistic budget, track expenses, and identify areas where you can reduce spending to free up resources for savings or debt repayment.
- Debt Repayment Plans: Develop a systematic plan for paying off debt, prioritizing high-interest debt and considering consolidation or negotiation options to lower interest rates or monthly payments.

Building Financial Resilience

3. Emergency Fund and Insurance

- Emergency Savings: Establish an emergency fund to cover unexpected expenses or financial emergencies, aiming for three to six months' worth of living expenses saved in a liquid account.
- Insurance Coverage: Ensure adequate insurance coverage for health, life, disability, and property to protect against financial risks and mitigate the impact of unforeseen events.

Strategies for Long-Term Financial Success

4. Investing in Education and Skill Development

- Continuous Learning: Invest in acquiring new skills, upgrading qualifications, or pursuing additional education to enhance earning potential and career opportunities.
- Financial Literacy: Improve financial literacy by educating yourself about personal finance, investing, and wealth-building strategies to make informed decisions and navigate financial challenges effectively.

Overcoming Psychological Barriers

5. Mindset and Belief Systems

- Positive Mindset: Cultivate a positive mindset and belief in your ability to overcome financial challenges, viewing setbacks as opportunities for growth and learning.

Conclusion

While financial obstacles may seem daunting, they also present opportunities for growth, learning, and resilience. By adopting proactive strategies, building financial resilience, and maintaining a positive mindset, you can overcome challenges, achieve financial stability, and ultimately realize your long-term financial goals. Remember that overcoming financial obstacles is not just about reaching a destination; it's about embracing the journey and empowering yourself to thrive in the face of adversity.

Retirement Planning and Wealth Preservation

Introduction

Retirement planning is a critical aspect of financial management that involves setting goals, implementing strategies, and making informed decisions to ensure a comfortable and secure retirement. As individuals approach retirement age, it becomes essential to preserve wealth accumulated over a lifetime and generate sustainable income to support their desired lifestyle during retirement. This guide explores key considerations and strategies for effective retirement planning and wealth preservation, empowering individuals to navigate this important phase of their financial journey with confidence and foresight.

Understanding Retirement Planning

1: Assessing Retirement Needs

- Lifestyle Goals: Identify your desired retirement lifestyle, considering factors such as travel, hobbies, healthcare expenses, and other discretionary spending.
- Income Sources: Evaluate potential sources of retirement income, including pensions, Social Security benefits, investment income, and other assets.

Creating a Retirement Plan

2: Developing a Comprehensive Retirement Plan

- Financial Goals: Set specific, measurable, achievable, relevant, and time-bound (SMART) financial goals for retirement, considering both short-term and long-term objectives.
- Asset Allocation: Determine an appropriate asset allocation strategy based on your risk tolerance, time horizon, and financial objectives, balancing growth potential with preservation of capital.

Generating Retirement Income

3: Sustainable Withdrawal Strategies

- Systematic Withdrawals: Implement a systematic withdrawal strategy, such as the 4% rule or dynamic withdrawal strategies, to generate consistent income while preserving the longevity of your retirement portfolio.

Wealth Preservation Strategies

4. Minimizing Tax Impact

- Tax-Efficient Withdrawals: Optimize tax planning strategies to minimize the tax impact of retirement withdrawals, including Roth conversions, tax-loss harvesting, and strategic asset location.

Estate Planning Considerations

5. Legacy Planning and Asset Transfer

- Estate Distribution: Develop an estate plan to ensure efficient transfer of wealth to heirs and beneficiaries, taking into account estate taxes, probate costs, and asset distribution preferences.

Conclusion:

Retirement planning and wealth preservation are ongoing processes that require careful consideration, proactive planning, and periodic review to adapt to changing circumstances and market conditions. By taking a comprehensive approach to retirement planning, including assessing retirement needs, developing a tailored retirement plan, generating sustainable income, and implementing wealth preservation strategies, individuals can achieve financial security and peace of mind during their retirement years.

Building a Legacy: Charitable Giving and Philanthropy

Introduction

Building a legacy through charitable giving and philanthropy is a noble endeavor that allows individuals to make a meaningful impact on society while leaving a lasting legacy for future generations. This guide explores the importance of philanthropy, the benefits of charitable giving, and practical strategies for maximizing the impact of donations. By embracing philanthropy as a core value and integrating it into their financial plans, individuals can create a legacy that extends far beyond their lifetime.

Understanding Philanthropy

1. The Power of Giving

- Impactful Contributions: Discover how even small donations can make a significant difference in addressing social issues and supporting worthy causes.
- Personal Fulfillment: Explore the intrinsic rewards of philanthropy, including a sense of purpose, fulfillment, and connection to the community.

Benefits of Charitable Giving

2. Personal and Social Benefits

- Tax Advantages: Learn about potential tax benefits associated with charitable donations, including deductions for cash contributions, appreciated assets, and charitable trusts.
- Enhanced Well-being: Understand how acts of generosity can improve mental and emotional well-being by fostering gratitude, empathy, and altruism.

Strategies for Effective Giving

3. Maximizing Impact

- Strategic Giving: Explore different approaches to charitable giving, such as targeted giving, collaborative partnerships, and impact investing, to maximize the effectiveness of donations.

Legacy Planning through Philanthropy

4. Creating a Philanthropic Legacy

- Mission and Values: Define your philanthropic mission and values to guide your giving strategy and ensure alignment with your personal beliefs and passions.
- Long-Term Impact: Consider establishing a donor-advised fund, charitable trust, or private foundation to create a lasting legacy and support charitable causes for generations to come.

Engaging Family and Community

5. Fostering Generosity

- Family Philanthropy: Involve family members in charitable activities and decision-making processes to instill a culture of giving and philanthropy across generations.

Conclusion

Building a legacy through charitable giving and philanthropy offers individuals an opportunity to make a positive difference in the world while creating a lasting impact that extends far beyond their lifetime. By embracing the principles of generosity, compassion, and social responsibility, individuals can leave behind a legacy that reflects their values, ideals, and commitment to making the world a better place.

Money and Relationships: Navigating Financial Conversations with Loved Ones

Introduction

Money plays a significant role in our lives, influencing not only our financial well-being but also our relationships with loved ones. Navigating financial conversations with partners, family members, and friends can be challenging, but it's essential for building trust, transparency, and mutual understanding. This guide explores the intersection of money and relationships, offering practical advice and strategies for discussing finances with loved ones effectively.

Understanding the Impact of Money on Relationships

1: Financial Dynamics in Relationships

- Power Dynamics: Explore how financial disparities can affect power dynamics within relationships and strategies for addressing imbalances.
- Communication Styles: Understand how different communication styles and attitudes toward money can influence relationship dynamics and conflict resolution.

Building Financial Intimacy

2: Cultivating Trust and Transparency

- Open Communication: Learn the importance of open and honest communication about finances, including sharing financial goals, values, and concerns.
- Financial Transparency: Discuss the benefits of transparency in financial matters, such as joint budgeting, shared financial goals, and regular money discussions.

Addressing Money Conflicts

3: Resolving Financial Conflict

- Conflict Resolution Strategies: Explore effective techniques for resolving money-related conflicts, such as active listening, compromise, and seeking professional help when needed.

Money and Relationship Milestones

4: Financial Planning for Couples

- Shared Goals: Discuss the importance of setting shared financial goals and developing a joint financial plan to achieve them.
- Life Transitions: Explore how major life events, such as marriage, buying a home, or having children, can impact financial dynamics and require adjustments to financial plans.

Supporting Each Other Financially

5: Financial Support and Boundaries

- Providing Assistance: Understand the nuances of providing financial support to loved ones and setting boundaries to maintain financial health and autonomy.

Balancing Independence and Interdependence

6: Financial Independence

- Individual Financial Goals: Emphasize the importance of maintaining individual financial goals and autonomy within the context of a relationship.
- Joint Responsibilities: Discuss strategies for balancing individual financial independence with shared financial responsibilities and goals.

Planning for the Future

7: Long-Term Financial Planning

- Retirement Planning: Explore strategies for long-term financial planning, including retirement savings, estate planning, and protecting financial assets for the future.

Navigating Financial Challenges Together

8. Overcoming Financial Hardships

- Support Systems: Discuss the importance of mutual support and resilience in navigating financial challenges, such as job loss, debt, or unexpected expenses.
- Seeking Help: Encourage open communication and seeking professional help when facing financial difficulties, such as financial counseling or therapy.

Celebrating Financial Milestones

9. Acknowledging Achievements

- Celebrating Success: Reflect on the importance of celebrating financial milestones and achievements together, reinforcing shared goals and accomplishments.

Fostering Financial Equality and Empowerment

10. Empowering Financial Decision-Making

- Shared Decision-Making: Encourage equal participation in financial decision-making processes, empowering each partner to contribute ideas, insights, and perspectives.
- Financial Education: Promote financial literacy and education within relationships, empowering partners to make informed financial decisions and build wealth together.

Conclusion

Money and relationships are deeply intertwined, and navigating financial conversations with loved ones is essential for building trust, transparency, and mutual understanding. By fostering open communication, cultivating trust, and supporting each other's financial goals and aspirations, couples and families can strengthen their relationships and achieve greater financial well-being together.

conclusion

In conclusion, navigating financial conversations with loved ones is a crucial aspect of building strong, healthy relationships. Money impacts various aspects of our lives, from daily decisions to long-term goals, and discussing finances openly can foster trust, transparency, and mutual understanding.

Throughout this guide, we've explored strategies for addressing money-related conflicts, setting shared financial goals, and supporting each other's financial well-being. By cultivating open communication, mutual respect, and a collaborative approach to financial decision-making, couples and families can strengthen their relationships and achieve greater financial success.

Remember, financial conversations may sometimes be challenging, but they are essential for building a solid foundation of trust and security in relationships. By actively listening to each other, expressing concerns and goals, and seeking professional help when needed, couples and families can navigate financial challenges together and build a brighter future.

Thank you for joining us on this journey to explore the intersection of money and relationships. May your financial conversations be filled with honesty, empathy, and shared aspirations for a prosperous future together.

THANKS FOR READING THIS BOOK

www.ingramcontent.com/pod-product-compliance
Lightning Source LLC
Chambersburg PA
CBHW051929210526
45473CB00006B/2192